the PET to GET

LIZARD

ROB COLSON

WAYLAND

First published in 2014 by Wayland
Copyright © Wayland 2014

Wayland
338 Euston Road
London NW1 3BH

Wayland Australia
Level 17/207 Kent Street
Sydney, NSW 2000

All Rights Reserved.
Editor: Annabel Stones

Produced for Wayland by
Tall Tree Ltd
Consultants: Camilla de la Bédoyère and Jane Hallam

ISBN 978 0 7502 8288 8

Dewey number: 639.3'95-dc23

10 9 8 7 6 5 4 3 2 1

Printed in China

Wayland is a division of Hachette Children's
Books, an Hachette UK company
www.hachette.co.uk

The publisher would would like to thank the following for
their kind permission to reproduce their photographs:

Key: (t) top; (c) centre; (b) bottom; (l) left; (r) right
(Shutterstock.com unless stated otherwise)

Front cover: Natali Glado; 1 Eric Isselee; 2 Lipowski Milan;
4 (c) Warren Price Photography; 5 (t) Muhammad Mahdi
Karim/Creative Commons; (c) Cathy Keifer; 6 (b)
blickwinkel/Alamy; 7 (c) Peter Krejzl; (r) tristan tan; 8–9
(c) Robert Eastman; 9 (t) Camilo Torres; 10 (c) Coy St.
Clair; 11 (t) kerstiny; (b) Exo Terra; 12 (c) SasinT; 13 (cl)
Lmnopg007; (c) Michal Durinik; 14 (cr) Steve Collender;
15 (t) Cathy Keifer; (c) Eric Isselee; 16 (b) D. Kucharski K.
Kucharska; 17 (t) Galina Barskaya; (c) Camilo Torres;
18–19 (c) Amwu/Dreamstime.com; 19 (t) Cinnamongirl/
Dreamstime.com; 20 sima-Zoran Simin; 21 (t) Ace Stock
Ltd/Alamy; (b) Juniors Bildarchiv GmbH/Alamy; 22 (b),
23 Cathy Keifer; 24 Robert Eastman; 25 (t) James
Christensen/Minden Pictures/FLPA (b) Julie Keen; 26 (b)
apiguide; 27 (t) Nneirda; (b) tratong; 28 Rommel Canlas;
29 (tr) Anna Kucherova; (tc) HANDOUT/Reuters/Corbis; (cl)
Mark Bridger; (cr) Martin Harms/Creative Commons; (cb)
Matt Jeppson; (br) reptiles4all; 30 (l) Robert Eastman (cl)
Amwu/Dreamstime.com; (cr) Eric
Isselee; (r) Cathy Keifer; (b)
Robert Eastman; back
cover: Istomina Olena.

CONTENTS

IS A LIZARD FOR YOU?

With their tough, scaly skin, lizards are unlikely to win a 'Most Beautiful Animal' contest, but they make fascinating pets. Watching how they grow and change will give you many hours of fun.

Basking in the sun warms lizards up and keeps them healthy.

COLD-BLOODED REPTILE

Lizards belong to a group of animals called reptiles, which are cold-blooded. This does not mean that their blood is always cold, but rather that it changes temperature with its surroundings. When it is cool, a lizard will slow down or go to sleep. It needs to lie in a warm place to give it the energy to move around.

CATCH ME IF YOU CAN

Lizards have a very clever way to escape from **predators**. They shed their tails and run away! You should never hold your lizard by the tail as it may shed it in panic. It grows back eventually, but losing its tail is very stressful for your lizard.

This white-headed dwarf gecko has shed its tail, which probably saved its life.

Most lizards eat insects. This chameleon is about to strike at a cricket with its long tongue.

THINK HARD

Before you buy your lizard, discuss it with your family. Think about how much time you can devote to your lizard, and be realistic. Some lizards can live for many years, so they are a long-term commitment. A chameleon will need checking a couple of times every day, while large lizards such as iguanas need plenty of space.

WHICH LIZARD?

There are more than 5,000 species of lizard and dozens of these can be kept as pets. Which you choose will depend on how much space you have and how much you want to handle your lizard.

HOW MUCH CARE?

Some lizards, such as the panther chameleon, need lots of care. Only buy a chameleon from a specialist breeder. They will give you good advice on keeping your lizard healthy.

SHOP CHECK

When you are in the shop or at the breeder, have a good look around to make sure the lizards are being cared for properly. The cages should be clean, with a fresh water supply, **full-spectrum** light bulbs and a covered heat pad. All the lizards for sale should be **captive-bred**, not caught from the wild. The shop should have written records to tell you when and where their lizards were born.

LOOKING HEALTHY

Make sure you choose a healthy lizard. It should be active and alert, with straight legs. Some signs of a weak animal include:

- bits of old skin stuck to the body;
- a lizard that is smaller than its cage-mates;
- a lizard that walks awkwardly;
- a lizard with no fat around the base of its tail.

Specialist pet shops such as this one have reptile rooms full of all kinds of species.

BAD BEHAVIOUR

Lizards are not always nice guys. If you keep more than one lizard, you may see one lying on top of the other. The one on top may be trying to dominate the one on the bottom. If they keep doing it, you may need to separate them. Keeping just one lizard is much easier than keeping two or three. However many you have, watch them carefully. The better you know your lizards, the faster you will spot when something is wrong.

HOW MANY?

You should never keep groups of male lizards together as they will fight one another. You can keep pairs of females but they may have health problems if they do not mate. It is often easiest to keep one male on its own. Lizards are mostly **solitary** animals so they will not get lonely.

A chameleon will need lots of attention.

BEARDED DRAGON FACTFILE

Bearded dragons take their name from the beard of skin under their mouths. They are medium-sized, friendly lizards that make excellent pets. If you buy one young, it will become tame very easily. These lizards can be handled regularly.

Soft spikes become prickly when it is frightened.

VIVARIUM

You will need a dry desert-style **vivarium** (see page 10). Use a **substrate** of bark chips or sand, and give your lizard rocks to climb on. These lizards like the heat, so the hottest end of the vivarium should reach **40°C**, with the temperature at **28°C** at the cooler end. At night, reduce the temperature to **20°C** and make sure it is dark, otherwise your lizard won't get to sleep. Full-spectrum lighting is essential to keep your lizard healthy.

IN THE WILD

Bearded dragons are native to Australia, where they thrive in hot, open **scrubland**. They also live in and around towns and cities. In the wild, bearded dragons sometimes live in family groups. If you keep more than one, watch how they act at feeding time. One of the lizards will be the dominant one and will always eat first. The others will wait their turn.

You'll need to give your bearded dragon live insects to catch. This female has caught a grasshopper with her sticky tongue.

A dragon's beard can change colour to make it more impressive. It puffs the beard out when threatened.

FOOD

Feed your dragon live insects, spring greens, flowers and the occasional **pink mouse**. Young dragons need mostly live food, fed to them every day. They reach adulthood at one year old. Adults should be fed every other day, and eat mostly plants.

HOME SWEET HOME

Lizards should be kept in cages called vivariums. It is very important to provide conditions in the vivarium that match the lizard's surroundings in the wild. This will keep it healthy.

This frill-necked lizard is warming itself on a log.

Many lizards are well **camouflaged**, making it hard for predators to spot them. This keeps the lizards safe while they warm up in the sun.

WET, FRESH AIR

The amount of water in the air is called **humidity**. Most tropical lizards will need high humidity and many lizards love being sprayed with water, too. The vivarium will also need good ventilation. Vent holes let fresh air in. Make sure the holes are covered in a fine wire mesh. This will stop any insects you feed your lizard from escaping into the rest of the house.

In the wild, bearded dragons drink from rock pools. Make sure there is always a supply of fresh water in the vivarium for your lizard to have a drink whenever it needs one.

WARM AND BRIGHT

Each species of lizard has its own heating and lighting needs. You will need a covered heat pad for your lizard to bask on, and a cooler area on the other side of the vivarium. Fit a **thermostat** to control the temperature. Most species of lizard also need full-spectrum light. A full-spectrum light mimics natural sunlight. Many lizards need natural light to make vitamin D, which keeps their bones healthy. Set the light on a timer to come on for 10–14 hours a day – your lizard will need some dark time, too.

You can buy fully fitted vivariums from a pet shop. This one is made of glass and metal, but you can also buy wooden ones.

HIDE AND SEEK

It is important to provide your lizard with places to explore and hide within its vivarium. This will keep the lizard safe and happy. The set-up of the vivarium will vary depending on the place the lizard lives in the wild.

SUBSTRATE

Whichever set-up you have, you'll need to cover the bottom of the vivarium with **substrate**. This is loose material such as sand, gravel or wood chips. Remove any substrate that contains droppings as soon as you see it, and replace it completely on a regular basis when you clean out the vivarium.

Bearded dragons live in deserts and hot woodlands. They need a hot, dry vivarium that also has things for them to climb onto.

DESERT SET-UP

Desert lizards need hot and dry conditions, but you also need to provide caves for them to retreat to. These will make cooler areas for the lizards when they have had enough of basking under the hot lamp.

SAFE PLACES

In the wild, lizards often hide in cracks in rocks, where they can cool down and feel safe from predators. Place objects around the vivarium to create hides for your lizard. You can make hides from lots of household things, such as plant pots, cardboard boxes or toilet roll tubes. Make hides in different spots so that your lizard can choose whether it wants to be warm and safe or cool and safe. Make sure there are no sharp edges that could injure a lizard.

This gecko feels safe looking out from its cave. You can make a cave like this using a flat rock balanced on two other rocks.

TROPICAL SET-UP

Tropical lizards love heat and humidity. Lizards such as chameleons and iguanas live in trees in the wild. They need a tall vivarium with branches to climb. Tropical lizards that spend lots of time on the ground, such as skinks, need rocks and cork logs to give them places to hide.

Lizards such as the plumed basilisk live in lush tropical forests in the wild. Their vivariums are like mini-jungles for them to explore.

Plumed basilisks live in rainforests in Central America.

LEOPARD GECKO
FACTFILE

Leopard geckos are named after the striking black spots on their backs that look like the spots of a leopard. They make a great first lizard as they are easy to keep and rarely get sick. You can train them to be handled if you start them young.

Wild habitat: Desert

Diet: Insectivore

Life expectancy: 20 years

Length: 20–22 cm

Ease of care: Easy

Geckos will eat flies – if they can catch them!

FOOD
Feed your gecko about every other day. A few small insects such as crickets are ideal. Leave them in the vivarium for the gecko to catch for itself.

VIVARIUM

Your gecko will need a desert-style vivarium with sand or wood chip substrate. You could add house plants to provide shaded areas. The temperature in the vivarium should range from 27–32°C, dropping to 21°C at night. Place the heat pad at one end. Leopard geckos are **nocturnal**, so they don't need full-spectrum lighting. Geckos are very clean and choose one spot to use as a toilet. Remove their droppings regularly, and clean out the vivarium every few months.

NIGHT SIGHT
Leopard geckos have large eyes to help them to see at night.

Leopard geckos store fat in their tails, which they live off in hard times. A gecko with a fat tail can easily survive a week without food.

IN THE WILD
Leopard geckos are hardy creatures that live in the rocky deserts of India and Pakistan. During the day, they avoid the blazing sun by hiding under rocks. They come out in the cool of night to hunt insects. Unlike most geckos, leopard geckos do not climb trees.

DINNER TIME

Lizards can eat a wide variety of food, depending on the species. Many eat just insects. Some are omnivores, and should be fed a mix of insects and leaves, while others just eat plants. You may also need to give your lizard **supplements** to keep it healthy.

INSECTS

Most lizards eat insects, and the insects need to be alive. Keep the insects for at least a day in a secure container with fruit and vegetables before feeding them to your lizard. This will make sure that the insects are themselves well-fed and full of **vitamins**. Stalking live prey will help your lizard to stay fit. Insects that make good lizard food include fruit flies, crickets, beetle grubs and locusts.

Mealworms are beetle larvae. They make a tasty occasional treat for omnivores such as bearded dragons.

MICE

Larger lizards, such as adult bearded dragons and chameleons, enjoy a small dead mouse as a treat. Savannah monitors will eat several mice in one go. You can buy mice from any pet shop. Keep them frozen and defrost them before serving. Smaller lizards might enjoy 'pinkies', which are small hairless mice.

SUPPLEMENTS

If you feed your lizard a good range of food, it should get all the vitamins it needs, but you can also buy supplements from the pet shop. Mix these in with their food according to the instructions. Ask a vet or experienced lizard keeper before using supplements.

Young iguanas eat insects, but adults only eat fruit and veg.

FRUIT AND VEG

Omnivores such as bearded dragons need a mix of insects and fruit and vegetables, while **herbivores** such as iguanas will live just on fruit and veg. Berries, salad leaves and flowers are favourites of bearded dragons, while iguanas love to tear into a whole apple. Put the food in a shallow tray away from the basking spot so that it does not dry out.

Bearded dragons love to munch on grasshoppers.

SAVANNAH MONITOR
FACTFILE

These large lizards are easy to keep if you have the space. They should be kept on their own in large vivariums. You need to beware of its potentially painful bite, and you may want to start with a smaller lizard before keeping a monitor.

Wild habitat: Grassland

Diet: Carnivore

Life expectancy: 10–15 years

Length: 100 cm

Ease of care: Experienced

VIVARIUM
You will need a large vivarium at least 2.5 metres long and 1.5 metres high. Add sturdy rocks and logs, and heavy water bowls. Give your monitor a sandy substrate about 30 cm deep – in the wild, these lizards dig burrows to hide away in, so it will want to be able to dig. The temperature should range from 28–32°C, dropping to 24°C at night when the lizard is asleep.

FOOD

Feed your monitor about twice a week, giving it as much as it can eat in five minutes. Young monitors should be fed insects. Adults will also eat whole mice. Scatter insects around the vivarium for the lizard to search out. This will make sure it gets enough exercise. It is important to keep your monitor active so that it does not become fat.

Young savannah monitors are a little lighter in colour than adults. They should be fed smaller insects.

Savannah monitors are most active at the start and end of the day, when temperatures are rising or falling.

IN THE WILD

Savannah monitors live in Africa, south of the Sahara Desert. Young monitors feed mostly on crickets. When they get bigger, they catch frogs and millipedes.

Savannah monitors use their sharp claws for digging and climbing.

LIZARD MATES

If your lizard gets used to being handled from an early age, it will become tame. You'll need to be gentle and to take your time. Remember that to the lizard, you are a giant. It will need time to learn to trust you.

HAND-FEEDING

Feeding your lizard by hand is a great way to gain its trust, but be careful of its bite. If you're feeding it insects, use tweezers. Lizards rarely bite, and if they do it's usually by accident. If you keep a large lizard, you may need to handle it with gloves. Ask the breeder for their advice when you buy your lizard.

This baby bearded dragon is eyeing up a piece of carrot.

Feed your lizard by hand while it is still young and it will grow up to be tame. But be patient and wait for the lizard to come to you.

This leopard gecko is tame enough to crawl on its owner.

HANDLING YOUR LIZARD

Give your lizard at least a week on its own to get used to its new home. Spend some time just watching it to learn how it behaves. When you pick your lizard up, place a hand under its stomach to support its weight. Make gentle movements so that you do not scare the lizard. Return it to its vivarium after a few minutes and offer it a tasty treat – it will start to link being picked up with being fed!

EXERCISE

Many small lizards will get enough exercise moving around inside their vivariums, but larger lizards can benefit from time outside their homes. In the wild, green iguanas regularly swim, and you can give your iguanas time in a plastic children's pool. Be sure to clean the pool thoroughly after using it. Some larger lizards can even be taken for walks using a special harness.

When they meet another lizard, many lizards will wave at each other. They are not being friendly – they do this to work out which lizard is the dominant one out of the two.

PANTHER CHAMELEON
FACTFILE

Chameleons are extraordinary creatures. They have skin that can change colour in an instant, eyes that move in all directions, and long tongues that shoot out at high speed. Panther chameleons need lots of care and it is best not to handle them, but the reward is that you get to watch their fascinating behaviour up close.

Wild habitat: Rainforest

Diet: Insectivore

Life expectancy: 4–7 years

Length: males 50 cm females 30 cm

Ease of care: Experienced

AMAZING TONGUE!
To see your chameleon's tongue in action, place food at different distances from it. The chameleon will shoot out its tongue to catch it. Blink and you'll miss it, as it all happens in a fraction of a second!

Male panther chameleons are larger and more colourful than females. Their colour changes according to the temperature and the mood they are in.

IN THE WILD

Panther chameleons live in the tropical forests in the north of the island of Madagascar, which is off the east coast of Africa. They are solitary animals that fiercely defend their territories from rivals.

Chameleons have pincer-like feet to grip branches.

VIVARIUM

In the wild, chameleons live in trees, so your vivarium should be high enough to have plants and branches for it to climb. The temperature range during the day should be 27–35°C, dropping to 22°C at night. You'll need full-spectrum lighting and to spray the vivarium every day – chameleons like to drink droplets of water from leaves. They must have moving air, so you'll need a small fan, but place it out of reach of the chameleon.

FOOD

Feed your chameleon on a wide variety of insects. They especially like flying and climbing insects. Young chameleons should be fed twice a day. They become adults at about 12 months old. Adult chameleons should be fed every other day.

HEALTH CHECK

If it is well cared for, your lizard should stay healthy for many years. However, you need to know what to look out for if it does become sick. Make sure you have the address and phone number of a vet who specializes in reptiles in case of an emergency.

A black beard shows that your dragon may be stressed.

KEEP YOURSELF HEALTHY

Lizards can carry diseases such as **salmonella** that can be caught by humans. You can make sure you don't catch anything by following these simple rules:

- Always wash your hands after handling a reptile.

- Clean the vivarium and everything in it once a month, and wear gloves while you do it.

- Clean any bites or scratches with an anti-bacterial cream.

This bearded dragon's beard has gone black, which means that it may be angry, wanting to mate or stressed. When this happens, it is best to leave it alone in its vivarium to calm down.

WHAT TO LOOK OUT FOR

Most of the diseases pet lizards suffer from are the result of poor care. Make sure that the vivarium is clean and at the right temperature, that you change the light bulbs regularly, and that you feed it the right diet. Pay attention to your lizard's habits, and you'll quickly notice when something is wrong.

Here are some of the things to look out for when you check your lizard:

- Is the skin colour becoming dull?
- Are its droppings smaller or harder?
- Are the legs swollen?
- Are there any lumps or bumps on its body?

Look out for changes in behaviour, such as staying in its hide for longer periods, or not climbing as much as it usually does. If you notice something wrong, have your lizard checked out by the vet.

Anoles are small lizards related to iguanas. This anole has a **tumour** on its back. If your lizard develops a tumour, you should take it to the vet.

If your lizard gets ill, it may need a visit to the vet. This bearded dragon is being given medicine through its mouth.

GREEN IGUANA
FACTFILE

Green iguanas are magnificent tree-climbing lizards. They feed on leaves, fruit and flowers. If properly tamed, iguanas can be handled, but they are big, powerful creatures and should be treated with care.

IN THE WILD

Green iguanas live in the tropical forests of Central and South America. They are found near lakes, rivers or the ocean, and are good swimmers. They are active during the day.

FOOD

Feed adults a wide variety of fruit, leaves and vegetables. Give it to them mixed up in a large bowl about every other day. Young iguanas also need some live food, so give them crickets or waxworms. Make sure there's a good supply of water. The iguana will leave droppings in the water, so clean it regularly.

Feeding time is crucial to tame your iguana. It is important for it to get used to being handled when it is still young, but make sure you keep your fingers out of biting range!

VIVARIUM

The vivarium will need to be a custom-built one or a special **reptile room**. Strong branches for climbing and basking are essential. Add plastic plants to provide shaded areas and cork logs to hide in. The daytime temperature range should be 25–30°C, dropping to 24°C at night, and a full-spectrum light is required. Your iguana will love being sprayed with water, but make sure it doesn't get too damp.

Green iguanas are big animals that need lots of space to roam.

GROWING OLD

Lizards can live long lives, but as your lizard grows older, it will slow down and spend more time resting. A lizard may need more care as it ages. Your vet can advise you how to care for an old lizard.

It is never easy deciding if it is time to have your lizard **put down**, but your vet will help you with this difficult decision.

Keep the best photos of your lizard so you can remember it. This crested gecko is giving its eye a good lick.

KEEPING A RECORD

To remember your lizard, it can really help to keep a record. Write down any notable events on a record card. You could make a scrapbook to keep photos, vet notes and any other documents you have for your lizard. Make a web page of your favourite photos and share it with your friends.

SAYING GOODBYE

Your lizard may die peacefully in its sleep or it may become ill and need to be put down by the vet. It is natural to feel sad when you lose your pet, but eventually your pain will pass and you wil be left with lots of happy memories.

AMAZING LIZARD FACTS

The largest lizard in the world is the fearsome Komodo dragon, which can grow up to 3 metres long. It preys on large mammals, such as pigs and deer.

The smallest lizard is the miniature chameleon Brookesia micra, which is just 25 mm long when fully grown. It is so small it can stand on the end of a match.

The Mexican mole lizard looks like a worm. It has no back legs, and uses its two clawed feet to dig its way through the soil like a mole.

The Texas horned lizard has an unusual and effective method of defence. If cornered, it squirts blood at its attacker from its eyes.

The Gila monster lives in the USA. It has a venomous bite, which it uses to kill prey. It is a slow mover, though, and prefers to feed on eggs.

LIZARD QUIZ

Test your lizard knowledge with this short quiz.

Can you identify these four different species of lizard from the photos?

1.

2.

3.

4.

5. Why do lizards shed their tails?

6. What do adult green iguanas like to eat?

7. Where are bearded dragons found in the wild?

8. Why do chameleons have pincer-shaped feet?

9. Why is it important to wash your hands after handling a lizard?

10. Why should you never keep males of the same species together?

GLOSSARY

CAMOUFLAGE
The use of colour and shape to blend in with the background. Lizards use camouflage to hide from predators.

CAPTIVE-BREEDING
The breeding of baby animals from parents that are being cared for by humans. It is vital to buy captive-bred lizards.

CARNIVORE
An animal that eats other animals.

FULL-SPECTRUM
Natural light that is produced by the Sun. Full-spectrum light contains ultra-violet rays, which we cannot see, but are important to keep many lizards healthy.

HERBIVORE
An animal that only eats plants.

HUMIDITY
The amount of water that is contained in the air. The water is in the form of a gas called water vapour.

NOCTURNAL
Active at night. Nocturnal lizards come out to hunt at night, when they are harder to spot by predators.

OMNIVORE
An animal that eats both other animals and plants.

PINK MOUSE (PINKIE)
A small, hairless mouse that some lizards like to eat. Pinkies are bought frozen from pet shops and thawed out before they are fed to the lizard.

PREDATOR
An animal that hunts and kills other animals to eat.

PUT DOWN
The ending of an old or sick animal's life by the vet. The animal is put down using a painless injection that peacefully sends it to sleep.

REPTILE ROOM
A room specially adapted to keep large reptiles such as iguanas.

SALMONELLA
A germ sometimes found on lizard skin that causes fever and stomach pain.

SCRUBLAND
An area in which small plants such as grasses and shrubs grow, but there are no trees. Usually scrubland is a semi-desert area with low rainfall.

SOLITARY
Living alone. Solitary animals spend most of their lives on their own and do not get lonely.

SPECIES
A kind of living thing. Members of the same species are able to reproduce with one another.

SUBSTRATE
The soft, loose material at the bottom of a vivarium.

SUPPLEMENTS
Additions to a reptile's diet that provide it with extra nutrients and vitamins.

THERMOSTAT
A device for controlling temperature. It ensures that the heater in a vivarium is turned on at the right times.

TUMOUR
A growth on the body of an animal. A tumour can be caused by cancer and may need to be removed.

VENTILATION
The way that air enters and moves around an enclosed area. A vivarium needs good ventilation, with new air constantly entering it.

VITAMINS
Chemicals that an animal needs to stay healthy.

VIVARIUM
A cage that a lizard lives in. Conditions in the vivarium are like those the lizard would experience in the wild.

USEFUL WEBSITES

www.thebhs.org
Website of the British Herpetological Society, devoted to reptiles and amphibians. Includes the Young Herpetologists Club for young people mad about reptiles.

www.nhm.ac.uk
Website of the Natural History Museum in London, with lots of information about all kinds of animals. Learn about how lizards live in the wild.

INDEX

the PET -to- GET

Is a ferret for you?
Choosing your ferret
Working ferrets
Living quarters
Wild cousins
Making friends
Playtime
Feeding your ferret
Keeping active
Showtime
On your marks!
Staying healthy
Growing old
Ferret quiz

978 0 7502 8292 5

Is a lizard for you?
Which lizard?
Bearded dragon
Home sweet home
Hide & seek
Leopard gecko
Dinner time
Savannah monitor
Lizard mates
Panther chameleon
Health check
Green iguana
Saying goodbye
Lizard quiz

978 0 7502 8288 8

Why a rat?
The right rat
Rats in the wild
Fancy rats
Moving in
Playtime
Dinner time
Great mates
Out and about
Health check
At the vet
Rat shows
Growing old
Rat quiz

978 0 7502 8289 5

Why a snake?
Which snake?
Corn snake
Snake house
Clean and healthy
Grey rat snake
Dinner time
Garter snake
Out and about
Ball python
Health check
Milk snake
Growing old
Snake quiz

978 0 7502 8290 1

Why a spider?
Which spider?
Spiders in the wild
A safe place
Chilean rose tarantula
Feeding your spider
Mexican red tarantula
Close encounters
The moult
Costa Rican zebra
Breeding spiders
Mexican blonde tarantula
Spider first aid
Spider quiz

978 0 7502 8291 8

WAYLAND